"Paul Dixon is not sa̶t̶i̶s̶f̶i̶e̶d̶ preconceived ideas of how others have done faith expressions in the past as 'successful.' This book calls us to become a part of flourishing neighborhoods, to listen deeply, seek God, become present to our context, de-clutter our lives, and see failures as opportunities. I love how he stresses the importance of us becoming pilgrims who invest our lives alongside the community that already exists, to build into the culture in which we are living, and to crave to be a part of the local culture. *Nomadic Faith* challenges us to be the hands and feet of Jesus in the world as we cultivate the soil of our soul, and to stop thinking that we have all the answers to the difficulties we face."

Mark Votava
Blogger and author of *The Communal Imagination: Finding a Way to Share Life Together*, member of the Tacoma Catholic Worker and Parish Collective Leaders Fellowship, a local practitioner in Downtown Tacoma, Washington.

"Paul Dixon simply and humbly invites the reader and church-planter to leave behind methods, number strategies and success-obsessed behaviour, and enter into a world that encourages one to just be and serve. Dixon opts for listening in lieu of performance, for material simplicity in lieu of busyness, and for relationships in lieu of Christendom's standards of church-planting success. Dixon dares to suggest that one listen, de-clutter, and seek out Holy Spirit designs as a way of living out *Missio Dei*. It is a tempting offer: At the end of the read, I thought, these are not lessons for church-planting; they are lessons for life."

Jenna Smith
Author of *A Way*

"Paul Dixon doesn't give us another 12-step book to church planting but gives us an understanding of why we plant churches in the first place: Loving God, building community, and the adventure of following God's voice on a faith-filled journey. Inspirational."

Marty Pronovost
Senior Leader at LifeHouse Humboldt

NOMADIC FAITH

Paul Dixon

Urban Loft Publishers | Portland, Oregon

Nomadic Faith

Urban Loft Publishers
2034 NE 40th Avenue #414
Portland, OR 97212
www.theurbanloft.org

ISBN-13: 978-0692299135
ISBN-10: 0692299130

Made in the U.S.A.

I dedicate this volume to my amazing wife who has stood with me in the thick of spiritual battle, challenged me to greatness and to be the man God has called me to be, and having the willingness to give me the space to do so. I also dedicate this book to my kids. I hope the lessons I write about in this book, which have become my ceiling in faith, will be the floor they stand on that propels them further then I could imagine in their journeys with our Father. I also want to thank the many people who had faith to give me the room to explore my faith and explore with me what it means to be the church.

Lastly I am ever grateful to my friend and publisher, Sean Benesh, who has the bravado to publish my writings, and the freedom to allow me to pour my heart out and share it with others.

To Him who can do who is able to do immeasurably more than all we ask or imagine, according to his power that is at work within us, to him be glory in the church and in Christ Jesus throughout all generations, for ever and ever! Amen.

CONTENTS

FOREWORD

When Paul first approached me to write this introduction, I had to confess that I had no clue how to proceed. I have known him for quite a while now, much of it through the electronic medium, but that didn't make the task any easier. You can know someone quite well, but when asked to write an introduction about him, it can often be hard to put your knowing into words. Paul and I go back to the moment he met his future wife while she played bass guitar in a worship team I was once part of on the east coast of Canada. I knew him when he moved to the middle of the country and really connected once he moved to the west coast. And as I reflected on our relationship, I marveled at how he has poured himself equally into his family and his calling, following the leading of God wherever it leads and whenever it comes.

Nomads follow the harvest ... and Paul is a nomad. He isn't afraid to move, to travel, to go where the fields are white for the harvest. Like the nomads of old who didn't lay down deep roots, Paul knows that the ability to go where the fruit is, to follow the herds, to engage the people in need where they are, that is what is essential for his identity. It is in him to reach people in this way, to uproot and travel and find the places where the harvest is plentiful.

There are not many people I know who can live a life like Paul has done. Between schooling, jobs, ministry opportunities, health issues, and family needs, he has located and relocated from one end of Canada to the other. We would trade emails and online conversations, commenting on each other's lives and actions, giving advice and a listening ear with each event, each crisis, each victory, each struggle. And every time he moved with his family I would wait for what I knew was the inevitable. Eventually a conversation would come from Paul that started something like this:

"Well, I was thinking about planting a church the other day ..."

And I knew the bug had got to him yet again. Nomads follow the harvest.

Church planting is more a reflection of who you are than what you do. It is a calling, a gift that is firmly grafted into your DNA. Regardless of who you are or what you do, it hovers in the background at all times, not quite out of sight, not quite out of mind. And no matter how hard you try to live a normal life, eventually it shows up and grabs you by the collar and stares you straight in the eyes. It is inescapable, a desire that cannot be satisfied by anything else. You can partner with others, you can sit on boards of outreach ministries, you can do missions, and you can share your faith with everyone you meet. But if you are called to plant, you are called to plant and nothing can fill this hunger to see new thriving groups be birthed and grown, and then pass them off to someone else so you can start afresh. It may seem strange, but that is just the way it is. It's even stranger for a nomad, for the location doesn't matter. You go where you are called, where you see a need, where you see a harvest. Birds gotta fly, fish gotta swim, planters gotta plant.

I thank God that there are people like Paul Dixon and his desire to plant. Partly because the way he is doing it seems so fresh and is yet so old. Partly because he connects with so many who may be considered by many as fringe believers but are rapidly becoming a growing pool from which a radical generation of new believers are springing. Partly because the type of planting and lifestyle he preaches and shares with those in his path show a dedication that many don't have. But mostly because I don't have to do it.

I have planted and helped plant a little in my time, but Paul and I see things differently. He is a radical, a new breed unashamed to be bold yet gentle at the same time. A man who will go anywhere, who finds his calling amongst those who make many of us scratch our heads and wonder if anyone could reach the world or impact another for Christ beneath the beard, the tattoos, and the strange clothes. I prefer the safety of the suburbs where the lost don't even know they are lost. Paul prefers the adrenaline routes of the streets or bike shops or avant-garde coffee bars or the off roads of bikers and X Gamers, people trying to fill an empty hole they don't know they have.

Paul feels the call to take the message wherever God leads him, however God leads him, whenever God leads him. This nomadic lifestyle of following the harvest flies in the face of a lot of our culture, but it is really a renewal of the old. It is how the gospel was spread so long ago, following the trade routes and caravans, reaching those whose home was wherever they were at that particular time. It was where salvation happened, it was where churches were born, it was where communities came together to worship. Dynamic, flowing, changing, radical, nomadic. Desert or city park, oasis or store front, trade route or bike trail, tent or coffee shop; it doesn't matter to someone like Paul. Regardless of our differences, what connects us is the same thing that connects us all: a God who loves and wants to meet us all, where we are, wherever that may be.

Nomads follow the harvest.

Jim Sutherland

Foreword

INTRODUCTION

Dear Church Planter,
Cling to Jesus tighter than your 'model.' The gospel is to be
your surest conviction.[1]

So you say you want to plant a church. Armed with stacks of books on the latest methods, strategies, market trends, you feel like you are ready to go. You have spent hours studying your city's demographics, strategically gathered the "right"people around you. You've hit up a few popular conferences and seminars, and now you are ready to launch out into your city to build a city-impacting faith community that will drive many people

---

[1] Acts 29 Europe. https://twitter.com/Acts29Europe/status/392323399080349696.

to the gospel, compel them to know Jesus, and offer aid to the poor.

You've found the answers and now it's "go" time. You start to plow forward, head down, and then look up when you have produced what seems like a church. After a period of apostolic fervor and applying academic methods, you feel able to pat yourself on the back, and put this church into cruise control. Time to take that much needed vacation after a couple years of hard work and allow the leadership team you disciple to take up the slack since they are ready to lead according to the DNA of what you sought to establish. Then you come back refreshed, with a renewed vision and excitement, ready to reproduce another church.

I once thought this way and I even tried it out. At one point in time, I figured that all the inspired reading material I could get my hands on was worth its weight in gold. I booked tickets to many popular conferences like Exponential and the ones Church Planting Canada put on (they were fun to attend!). I knew the calling on my life, and I was ready to go once I sensed God said "Go."

But then came a small whisper, "Be still and know that I am Lord."[2] I was taken aback, my readiness was thwarted. But I tried to move forward anyway. After meeting roadblock after roadblock, seeing doors close before they opened, I began to wonder what was happening. After all the books I had read, attending all the right conferences, and listening to the best podcasts on church planting, I was still not successful by any standard that was laid out before me.

Again came that small whisper: "Be still and know that I am Lord." This time I took heed. I waited. I listened. I put aside the stacks of information, the notebooks I had written in, I stripped away my efforts, and let God speak. I came to realize that he had a plan, he had ideas, he had places where he was already working in the city. It was my job to be still, and let God do the talking and leading. He is Lord, I am not. He knows how he wants to reach a particular place and particular people. I wanted to run, but I could barely crawl. I wanted to do great things for Jesus, but in my own strength.

Our missional endeavors are not our own. We are sent by God into the world to make disciples, to guide people to get closer, deeper, more intimately connected to him.

---

2 Psalm 46:10.

Since it is God who is sending us, then it makes sense for us to allow his Spirit within us to be our guide. We need to submit ourselves, lay aside our ideas, and let God be in control. He has plans for us to prosper, as we move forward into a tribe, people group, urban core, and community, to spread his love and grace as we know it to be through the gospel.

It is God who sent the disciples to spread the good news. They did what Jesus had modeled for them, to follow the Spirit, let him be the guide of each footstep they took, share the strategy, build the plan, and move them into the relationships they needed to be in. Essentially they allowed the Holy Spirit to reveal the mind of Christ to them as they sought to reach out to the places they went.

"Since we live by the Spirit, let us keep in step with the Spirit" (Gal 5:25). God placed the Holy Spirit in us to be our guide and counselor, and a reminder that he is with us. So let us put aside ourselves, cast off our ways, and allow God from within us to give direction, to guide us forward to see faith communities birthed, to see people enter into or be renewed in the relationship of love and intimacy that God desires with them. Deny yourself, take up your cross, and follow him (Mark 8:34).

Ask the Holy Spirit for permission to go, to bless and send us, to consult with him continuously along the pathway of your pilgrimage to see the gospel take root in people's lives. Let's pick up the cross, and allow Holy Spirit to be your guide in every step. Take the time each day (in fact many times each day) to pray, seek direction, ask for wisdom, and follow him. We need to possess the bravado in faith to follow through in action with what God via Holy Spirit is sharing with us. Make time in your busy life to cultivate a deep personal relationship with the Shepherd so like sheep we will know his voice when he speaks.

It's time we learn to allow the seemingly silent partner to speak, guide, and direct us toward building his kingdom. Resting in his presence, letting him speak love and guidance to us, is the single most important step for all of us who aspire to birth new faith communities and impact lives with the gospel of Jesus. Let's dig in together, press the reset switch, put our phones in airplane mode and give Holy Spirit the time to speak into us. Then take the time to put into action the words we hear in our prayers. Become the hands and feet of Jesus to the place he has sent you under guidance by Holy Spirit. I know that as we do this we will be pleasantly surprised at how discipleship moves forward, how gatherings of the church begin to blossom into deep communities that resemble Jesus' bride, and how we grow deeper in intimacy with Abba, our heavenly daddy.

With that thought in mind:

Open the eyes of our hearts, Lord, so we can see where you are leading, and see how you want your church to form and grow within the context you are calling us to. Give us wisdom to always seek you first. I pray that we never grieve and shut down your Spirit within us. Holy Spirit, we want to know you more, more deeply, more intimately. You have the freedom to speak to us. Thank you for the call on our lives to go into the world and share the gospel. Be our guide, our Lord, our Savior.

In Jesus' name. Amen.

CHAPTER I
Follow Me

"Each church should hear the call from God as to what they are or aren't to be."[1]

There was an evening a couple years ago when I found myself sitting cross-legged on a living room floor, a wide-mouth mason jar in hand filled with delicious whiskey. Around the circle were some of life's vagrants, bike messengers, mechanics, hippies, social activists, all coming together to hang out united by a mutual love of bicycles. So there I sat amongst them; a couple were my friends, but many were new faces. In this group setting as I was sitting sipping my whiskey, I had the joy to share

---

[1] Halter, *Tangible Kingdom*, 113.

about the hope I had in my life, to offer them a glimpse of the gospel. Maybe it was the whiskey talking that gave me the bravery to speak, but it was also Holy Spirit speaking through me into their lives.

I knew I was supposed to go to this house party. Normally it's not my scene, yet a couple I had become friends with quickly since moving to that city had invited me to come along. There was a prompting deep in me to go, to meet new people, that I had to be at this event even though it was a going away party for someone I didn't know. A thought crossed my mind that I would get a chance to speak to some about Jesus, about why he is important to me. The very idea fought against the legalism I perceived had been my upbringing—"Come on, fella Whiskey and Jesus?!" Seriously it was a struggle. But I knew I had to be there. To steal a phrase from pop Pentecostal circles, "I knew that I knew that I knew" that I was supposed to go. There was a holy nudge. So I agreed to go.

Fast forward back to the scene at the house on the living room floor. I began to share about my experiences with faith, my love for the church, and how I knew Jesus loved those people. The more I spoke, the more the partygoers gathered around. The bottle of whiskey slowly began to empty, the night began becoming early morning. It was time to head home to sleep off the whiskey and brush my teeth so that when my wife kissed me in the morning she didn't need to experience the breath that accompanies Famous Grouse. As I fell asleep, in my spirit I heard, "Well done, good and faithful servant."

What happened was a sacred time that could only have been orchestrated by a God who is everywhere. He took a fool like me, who seems to need a few shots of liquid confidence before he has the bravado to share any aspect of the gospel, and spoke through me into the lives of others. I had to be willing to follow his leading that evening, to go to a strange house with folks I didn't know (they eventually became a beautiful and treasured group of friends to me as our relationships grew), in order for them to encounter God.

In the long term, did it birth a church? No, but it was a moment of time where I was able to help those who sat around me come on a journey that was safe, to see their hearts open up and their spirits laid out and open to the gospel. They were thirsty, and I was leading them closer to the eternal, to the living water that makes them thirst no more. That night we all took a sip from the well just as the Samaritan woman had, and we came away changed by our time with Jesus.

I have had many more experiences like this one, which rocked the strongholds of my conservative theological mind as I tried to push past the religiosity of my past into the true religion of love that God has called me into by his grace, and with which he sent me into the world. I can tell stories that I barely remember (likely because of too much beer) of being in pubs praying with random people and seeing the Holy Spirit speak through me to them, and releasing them of their illnesses both physical and spiritual. One time a fellow walked into the pub on crutches, and left after some prayer time not needing them! (Yay Jesus!) These times happened because I became a willing child of God. I go to whom and to where the Holy Spirit would take me, and I watch the power of the gospel roll from my lips and pierce the hearts of those around me.

There is a beautiful old ritual said to be from Scotland. When someone comes to your home you open the door holding a *quiach*, a two-handled cup that cradles whiskey. As a symbol of peace and hospitality you pass the cup to your guest for a sip. In those moments of life when Holy Spirit speaks through me to others, I have in my hands a holy *quiach*, a mug filled with the gospel and I am handing it off to the person in front of me for a sip of the kingdom of God.

This is missional church planting. It's messy, it grates against the theological systems of our upbringing, we end up where we may never have expected to be, and yet it changes us as much as it changes the people we are sharing God with. We need to learn to get out of the way and allow the Holy Spirit to be the guide. We need to put down the models modeled to us, because what has worked for others isn't necessarily meant for us to use. Instead we need to turn our eyes to God, sit at his feet, and ask him what he wants.

In these times we learn to lean on his strength instead of our weakness. As you sit with me, also with a jar of whiskey, fighting against the religion and legalism that binds your mind, and you see how in the moment as we lay aside our presuppositions, there is a place where God shines through, where his strength comes out and he shares his love with those he loves. You become a missionary in that moment.

Go on. Take a sip of whiskey with me, have the bravado to put down the books, to step away from the table where you fill yourself on the latest trends, "proven" methods, and the baggage of your past. Let me pass you the holy *quiach* and take a sip. God is offering you so much more, speaking to you in a deeper way. In that holy *quiach* is living water. Are you brave enough to take a sip? Do you possess enough faith to step away from the table and allow Holy Spirit to guide your steps, to take you on a magic carpet ride?

Learning to follow Holy Spirit into the unknown, into the promised land where he wants you to be, to a particular place and time, to a particular people, is not a new idea. Dropping our ideas, philosophies, and religiosity, to let God lead us, move us, shake us, to let him be King in our life, is a very old idea. People have struggled with this since the beginning of time. Even in the Garden and in the opening chapters of the Bible we see people facing the challenge of surrendering their lives to follow God. One of my favorite examples is the people of Israel, who tried hard to live together as a society, tried to learn to live to the letter of the law, wanting to know where, when, and how God was going to lead them into the promised land. They went through some horrendous times where others guided them according to strict rules and regulations. They were slaves to the harsh laws their priests were trying to enforce on them as God's chosen people.

God broke through all of that, all their past history and experience, their slavery, and their trying to understand what's next. Israel was trying to figure out their path through the wilderness, craving what they did not have. Then God offered a sign to the people that was not just seen by a few, but by everyone. God offered them clear guidance. God broke past the routine, the normalcy of what was happening and said, "Follow me."

Deep in the deserts the Israelites were camped, desperately trying to develop a civilization and culture after God had rescued them from their Egyptian captors, hoping to find the promised land. Weary from all the walking, their feet ached, their minds were confused, and they craved real sustenance. So they set up a tent as a makeshift temple where the priests could enter into the presence of God. They went into this quiet, sacred place with hopes that God would offer guidance, tell them their next steps, all the while hoping that he would lead them to the promised land.

Once the tent was set up, God covered it with his presence in the form of a cloud. When the cloud lifted up and began to move, the priests summoned the Israelites to do the same, to pack up and move, following the cloud to the next destination God had prepared for them. "This is how the Eternal One indicated when the Israelites should travel and where they should set up camp."[2]

The Israelites were learning a valuable lesson, to follow the presence of God. In their case it was a pillar of cloud. So it is with us; as Christians, we too must learn to follow the pillar of cloud. It should be our deepest desire to seek the presence of God and to follow him into the mission he has called us to.

"Come follow me," Jesus cried out. He was the presence of God to the disciples; where he moved so too did the disciples. He would send them out at times with his presence, Holy Spirit, as their guide. They didn't have a tangible cloud to follow; the cloud—the Spirit-was in them. The same is true for us as well. We need to dig deep, cultivate the soil of our soul, and remove the weeds so that we can follow Holy Spirit with clarity. He moves us through our nomadic faith, on a pilgrimage that takes us ever closer to the Father, and out into the world to the people he loves.

---

[2] Numbers 19:18.

"I will ask the Father to send you another Helper, the Spirit of truth, who will remain constantly with you." Jesus proclaimed to his disciples, as well to us. "You do know the Spirit because He lives with you, and He will dwell in you."[3]

God has given us the Great Commission, as it is popularly called, to go into all the world, to baptize and make disciples, as well to heal the sick, cast out demons, speak with new tongues, and drink poison without being harmed.[4] But how do we know where to go? How do we know to whom we are sent? What is our strategy?

This is how it should be. God gave us a cloud, Holy Spirit, to follow into the harvest, to find the people he is working with already, through whom we will see faith communities develop (persons of peace as some call them), as a result of which people will become disciples, neighborhoods will flourish, and cities will be blessed.

Jesus calls to the disciples, to us, "Follow me."

---

[3] John 14:16,17.

[4] Mark 16:15-18.

We hesitate and rebut "But, Jesus, what's the plan? I've got 10 steps here of what we are to do and you want me to put that aside?!" "I have just learned this great way to plant a church based on so-and-so's book, and I spent a fair amount of money going to that conference recently."

He replies, "Put aside your strategies and ideas, and follow me." Jesus beckons us to believe, "I will be your guide. I will show you the way, the steps to take, how I want this church to be."

There is more to life than following a set of rules that prevents us from moving forward, from going side to side, unless we stay within the lines. Such is how it seems many approach church planting. We think there are rules, defined strategies, ways that things have to be done. Our checklist is prepackaged; it determines the steps we need to take, the documents we need to produce and fill out, how to apply for tax-free status and become a charity, and how to share the gospel. The checklist assumes one size fits all.

Ed Stetzer, a popular missiologist and church planter, says, "When we adopt a pre-packaged church formula, or simply steal another church's identity, we often import the vision God has given someone else for a certain time and place and make it ours—we import a model rather than engaging in God's mission."[5]

As a child, I used to love playing with Lego. What I could build out of those boxes of random pieces was only limited by my imagination. The possibilities were endless. I spent hours creating scenes, buildings, vehicles, and many other things. What came from my hands were products of my imagination that looked authentic to me. Nowadays those random kits seem hard to find; in their place are boxes with instructions, with specific parts that are limited to building only one thing. It seems if you miss a step or lose a piece the kit is useless. With these kits I can build an X-wing, a race car, Hogwart's castle, and even Mordor.

It's the same with church planting. No longer do we need to listen to God and let our imaginations run wild with his; we can carefully follow the steps to build our Lego churches. We can choose to follow the kits, be they Willow Creek, Elevation, Saddleback, Mar's Hill, or whatever else is out there.[6]

---

[5] Stetzer, "Do Not Plant or Pastor a Church in Your Head."

[6] Surratt, "The Danger of Planting Lego Churches."

I am guilty of this. After reading the many books on strategy that line my shelves and fill up my Amazon Kindle, the how-to's on starting a church, magazine articles that share the best new methods and sage words of wisdom from the Jedi masters of church planting, I had created a confined box of how to do it. My checklist was made, my forms were filled out, and I was ready to move forward into a successful church plant. Yet there was one piece missing, one very important thing that I and others had ignored: Holy Spirit. Oh yeah, that guy! Our constant companion, who loves to tell us God loves us, who loves to offer guidance and counsel, who wants to draw us back to the boxes of random parts and guide us on how to assemble them.

"The wind blows wherever it pleases. You hear its sound, but you cannot tell where it comes from or where it is going. So it is with everyone born of the Spirit" (John 3:8).

What if we were to drop all our preconceived ideas, theologies, and strategies, and take time to listen to God, to listen to what he wants for his church and how we should move forward with that? How different would our efforts look?

Recently in a service at the church I currently attend a man shared his story and struggles with us. He spoke of how Jesus appeared in a vision on the hood of the coal truck he was driving down a tight mountain road. Jesus poured out affirmation and love on him, then spoke a word about this man's future. With clarity, Jesus, revealed his strategy for how he wanted a church to be planted, where it was to be, its core values, and many other details. Jesus had the plan, the who, the where, and the way to do it. "Follow me," he called out to his disciple.

In accordance with this man's faith, he listened to the call of God, packed up his belongings and family, and moved to the place Jesus had told him to go to. He then sought God daily to find out what was next. The openness of this humble man lead to God providing opportunities to share the gospel, gather others in the area to begin meeting together, form a community, and journey together on a pilgrimage to see a new faith community develop. Through this man's willingness to follow Holy Spirit, a faith community was birthed. Certainly each day came with challenges and spiritual warfare (a topic we'll address in a later chapter), but he pressed in because God called him to that place, to those people, and to the work he had already begun.

In a recent film (*Father of Lights*) there is a scene where a missionary speaks of how God wakes him up at four every morning to give him his marching orders for the day. He seeks the Spirit within, so that he can follow where he would lead him. Sometimes the orders are clear, other times a new level of alertness. For example, there is a village hidden across from a water pump at the end of a bridge. Interestingly the man had been on that particular bridge many times and had never seen the pump beside it. Faithfully this man rises and follows God to the hidden village. As a result of this man's faithfulness to God's revelation, the people God intended should hear his gospel that day heard it, and churches began to form and grow in a village that previously didn't have them. He even saw a witch doctor disappear from the village. All because this man had enough bravado within to put aside himself and let God do the leading.

I feel a conviction deep within me that if it is God who is sending us on mission, then it is to God we should turn to and ask how he wants it done. He gave us our cloud, Holy Spirit, to lead us to where the work in the field is to be done. Sometimes He may point us to a particular book, sometimes he may come in angelic form, or he may whisper within our minds to reveal his plans.

Regardless of how our mission is provided to us, we should go first to the source of all life, God. Through prayer and reading Scripture we will learn to hear God's voice speaking to us and we will gain God's insight for his church, and to where Holy Spirit will lead us.

Chapter I: Follow Me

CHAPTER II
Unclutter Your Life

Zombies! There all around us, clued-out to the world around them, focused on one particular thing: their phones. Clumsily stumbling about, fixated on their all-important apps, annoying others around them with its beeps, blips, and the odd sight of them seemingly talking to themselves because we can't see their Bluetooth ear bud. But it's just one of many, many, distractions in our world that zone many of us out. How about that idiot box, aka the TV, that shrine to the god of entertainment in your living room?

Turn it off, put it away. Yes, you know I'm referring to your smart phone, your laptop, your TV, and head to your quiet place. How can you expect to have a quiet time with your Daddy if those notification beeps are constantly going off? The most important task on your to-do list is to spend time in the presence of God.

I find one of the greatest features on my phone is the airplane mode. It allows me to shut down everything with the flick of a button. Voila! My digital leash has been cut. Next I close the lid of my laptop and walk away from the temptations of the information superhighway, and the false urgency of Instagram, Twitter, Facebook, and any other social media distraction so I can form the perfect online profile giving an epic indulgence into adventure, and showing off how spiritual I am. Even in public spaces I will do this, partly out of respect for those around me, but also so I can focus on those in front of me.

One of my favorite games to play when going out with friends is "the bill game." Everyone places their phone in a pile on the table; the first one to grab their phone from the pile to respond to a beep before the meal is over pays. Try it. You might be surprised how many coffees and meals your friends get to pay for, provided you have the willpower to not grab your phone before they go for theirs.

If I am sent into a noisy world, say to a great local cafe to pray and seek God, then why am I choosing to add to the noise that is already around me distracting my attention? (Unless of course it's like now as I sit in the "office" to work on this book.) All that's usually in front of me on the table is a pen and paper, as well a delicious coffee, so I can stay alert while I write down what I hear God sharing with me. As well, if I happen to overhear people sharing their hurts, those become my prayer requests. I write them down, and sometimes if the Spirit leads me, I will go and ask that person if I can pray for them.

"A key factor with many of us is that our lives are too complex and too busy. We simply don't have time. Does life have to look like a rat race or exhausting treadmill? I don't think so. Five years ago I wrote about being too busy not to evangelize, and I followed up with some ways to create missional margin in your life. Woody Allen once said that 80% of success is just showing up. We need to be present, and present with a purpose to live with others, love them, and lean into the kingdom under the leadership of the Spirit to magnify Jesus," says Tim Brister in a well-written blog post.[1]

---

[1] Brister, "5 Simple Ways to Move from Strangers to Missionaries."

In our urban settings it is hard to find a quiet place. Living in a smaller urban center I am blessed with fewer people living busy lives, as well as some great parks to go pray in. I really love this one park on a hill in the center of the city, I can bike up to the peak, ride around and enjoy some simple single-track trails, and take in the beauty of God's creation. But also I can sit on a rock ledge that overlooks the entire city and pray for it. There are days when I am strongly convicted by Holy Spirit to do this (it's important to pray over the city in which you've been placed). Other days he leads me to a busy street to sit and soak in the noise of the urban world around me, and to pray for his presence to infiltrate the lives of the people bustling around me. But unless I take the time to turn my focus to God, I might miss the chance to be blessed, and be a blessing to others.

We need to set aside Sabbath days, and put ourselves on an information fast. There are so many binary beeps around that arouse our neurons and whisper sweet new ideas to us, that we can easily lose focus. With 22 browser tabs open, a Kindle full of new books, and my smart phone (proudly not an iPhone, I'm with Android all the way) beside me constantly beeping notifications of new incoming info, I find it hard to not immerse myself in stuff to massage my brain with. Yet a task is at hand on my Sabbath, and that's escape technology, write a book, and take time to listen to what God is telling me to put down on paper.

When I manage to take some uncluttered, disconnected time to delve into prayer, to soak in God's presence, I always feel refreshed and full of joy. I do find one tool very useful. That tool is a notepad. I rest it beside me as I pray, and write down those random thoughts that pop into my head, to-do list items, new ideas, solutions to problems, and people I need to contact. By releasing those thoughts quickly to paper so I remember them later, I can turn my focus back to God. Sometimes the list becomes a list of names of people God has brought to me to pray for, or a place he wants me to go. I try to make this time a habit, yet it's quite hard considering my addiction to technology (you should see the hours I have wasted reading websites in my pursuit of a new smart phone and bicycles).

In my home it is hard to be uncluttered and find time to focus on God and his voice. I have four amazing kids running around, two toddlers, a preschooler, and a seven-year-old son. I am constantly coming up with ideas for building projects. The result is our home can become more noisy than the streets that surround our downtown core. Sometimes I have to wake early in hopes of having a quiet time, hoping they'll sleep in for a while. But this doesn't often happen in my house (reality check: kids don't sleep in). At other times I head to the reading room with Scripture in hand (if you are a parent, you understand what I mean) to take care of business. As my kids get older and become involved in sports and other programs, I know the noise will shift from loud playtime and crying for bottles to racing around to get them places on time and over to friends' houses for play dates. And yet even in the midst of all this, we can find time to be uncluttered, to put aside our digital media and rest in knowing God is Lord, and let him pour into us his love, his plans, and his gentle correction.

Often we think that this quiet time is the least productive part of our day. "You mean you just sit and listen, or possibly meditate on some Scripture?" some people ask. Yes, that's what I do. What I have come to learn as a church planter is that the most important and most productive time of each day is when I put my day and the needs of those I love before God, and ask him how I can impact other people's lives according to his desire. I know this is also true for friends who are Average-Joe Christians seeking to live out their day for God. I am often humbled by knowing my mother-in-law (who lives in our basement) is up each morning reading Scripture and praying for our family before she heads off to work. It's a beautiful discipline.

It seems we tend to heed too much the voice of the world that tells us busy-ness adds value to our lives. We only have one life to live, this voice says, and we need to cram in as many things as we can. Our to-do lists become packed with nagging things need to get done, goals we want to achieve, and a bucket list of adventures we crave. When we focus on the noise of life, God gets too easily tuned out, and we miss out on his beautiful words whispered into our souls. Words that will give us breakthrough to the next step in the mission God has called us to.

So please try this: Put away your devices, put your phone on airplane mode, and find a still quiet place and allow God to speak to you. I know it may seem silly having to tell you this, but we all need a reminder at times, including myself, to do this. Unclutter. Make time in your life for God. Even in our noisy urban environments, we can find space for God, a place where we can hear his voice leading us to the field he wants us to harvest alongside him.

There is a second part to uncluttering your life. There are other noises we need to put away, push past, and not let get inside our cranial space and influence us. The other day I was wrapping up a prayer time with a friend, a fellow planter, actually the guy who I am journeying with currently to plant a missional-focused church in our city. We had a powerful prayer time together, and then I had to hop in my purple people-transporter (I really wanted to say "purple people-eater" – great song!), aka the mini van, and head back home. As soon as I got in the driver's seat, buckled in and started the van, God spoke. He reminded me of all the times growing up that I heard "Paul does not live up to his potential."

Yea, I heard that a lot. In some ways I took pride in it, especially in regards to parent-teacher interviews at school. It meant I wasn't in trouble with bad grades, but usually got spoken to about pulling up my socks (sometimes I would literally do that while being lectured). That statement became, unbeknownst to me, a mantra of how I slid through, how I glided down the easy path, not pushing myself hard, but seemingly doing well. Does not live up to his potential. In that moment in the van, my heart was prepared and opened to receive some personal stuff. After intense prayer, God spoke, pulled up some clutter from deep within me and wanted me to cast it out.

As I write this now I hear God speaking. He's pulling my mind back to a time when I was told of my God-given potential. I was in New York City, entering a homeless shelter where I would spend the next two weeks helping out. I was with leading a team of youth that I brought with me from my local church to help shape them by experiencing missions. I digress. I entered the homeless shelter. And as I stepped over the threshold the director met me and another member of our team. Immediately he spoke, telling me he had seen me in a dream last night, and that he had a word for me: "There was an apostle named Paul; you will do greater things then he did." For years this word has haunted me, but in the beauty of this moment, God connected that to my experience of him pulling out the old mantra, "does not live up to his potential."

There is no question in my mind this mantra has guided me for far too long. It likely influenced the amount of effort I put into other church plants I was involved in. I felt unconsciously that I was not living up to, and not living out, my God-given potential. That is the other clutter in our lives; it's deep, it's spiritual, it's at the core of our being, and it has become our guiding principle whether we recognize it or not.

It's the notifications that beep on a core level within us. They too need to be silenced; they too need to stop taking our attention away from the task at hand. Let's be realistic. We all have heard the condemning comments. They have attached themselves to us and become nestled deep in our inner being. Without our realizing it, they guide us. Beep. Beep. Beep. They are trying to grab our attention and guide our decision-making, guide how we speak and live out the gospel in the context we've been sent to. They need to be silenced. These beeps of spiritual notifications can't be turned off by hitting the airplane mode. Such a thing unfortunately does not exist.

It's not going to be silenced that easily. But when we go to God with those distractions, he can silence them by speaking the truth to us. The beeps can only come out through time with God, through prayer, when we sit down enter his presence and allow him to turn off and more importantly remove those squeaky chains weighing down our life. God takes care of it; he applies the chain lube, he cleans us up, shines us up, and puts the lubricant right where it needs to be. He wants to tear out the mantras that beep and squeak, and replace them with wondrous divine truth: "There was an apostle named Paul, and you will do greater things then he."

This is the other side, the spiritual side, to uncluttering our lives. It takes bravado to sit at the feet of Jesus, and let him speak love into us as he pulls out these painful things that have been guiding us with a voice louder than that of Holy Spirit within us. So please sit up, put in your trays, put your electronic devices on airplane mode, and let Jesus be your guide, your Savior, your King.

CHAPTER III
Pushing Forward

As we move forward, pushing open wider the gates of the kingdom of Heaven, naturally we are also painting a target on our backs, some great big circles with a little bull's-eye in the middle. Each step we take to incarnate Jesus to others offends Satan, who hopes to take us out aiming right for the bull's eye. This is important, very important, to consider. What am I talking about? Spiritual warfare. It's a reality that will happen as we seek to breathe the life of God into people, into neighborhoods, and into new faith communities. Be prepared always for the reality of spiritual warfare.

Seeking Holy Spirit is very important at this stage. I have countless stories of attacks, of Satan trying to take me out of the game as I sought to follow God on mission and plant churches. I recall vividly the last plant I led. Shortly into the process of forming a core group, I had health issues that brought into question my ability to keep working bi-vocationally. I really valued the idea of being bi-vocational because it kept me connected with the larger community; it gave me a practical way to present the gospel. However, I lost my job. A sharp pain had rapidly developed in my wrists, and the loss of strength was too great for me to continue working as a bicycle mechanic. It hurt too much to turn wrenches, and I was not able to safely tighten bolts any more. Also along with the pain came the beginnings of some kind of chronic fatigue. I became unreliable as an employee.

A further example of spiritual attack occurred at the same bike shop where I worked. There was an incident involving a co-worker who was clearly demon-influenced. While I was truing some wheels and making adjustments on a bike for a customer, my co-worker threw a large bike at me while my back was to him. It hit me and knocked me to the ground. Then he yelled at me, asking why I didn't move out of the way. As a Christian shouldn't I be able to foretell what is going to happen to me? I looked at him and could see a deep blackness in his eyes. This usually caring, happy fellow was not himself. It was clear that something had grabbed hold of him that had caused him to try and unnerve me, to scare me from ever presenting the gospel in this bicycle shop. I also had a hard time finding favor with other co-workers once they were aware of my faith and that I was trying to start a church.

Within the same week of losing my job due to my growing illness, things began randomly to break down such as computers, appliances, and vehicles. Personality conflict rose to epic levels within the community house we lived in. There were 12 of us living under one roof sharing life together (mostly), and some major personality conflicts surfaced that messed up the atmosphere of our home. Hang-out times that once were sweet with worship turned into conflict management.

Members of our church plant felt the effects as well. They faced some of the same challenges that were trying to take us out of the game. They had vehicle issues, family fights, and new health problems. These are some of the realities that likely will happen to you and your disciples and team as well. I don't mean to scare you, but simply to make you aware of the spiritual battle we are part of. Remember it's not flesh and blood we battle against, but powers and principalities.[1]

---

[1] Ephesians 6:12.

I can not reiterate or plead with you strongly enough of the importance of prayer, and listening to Holy Spirit as our guide and comforter. Prayer is our weapon. We need to do more than put on the full armor of God as Paul describes in Ephesians 6. There is another important part of warfare. That key piece is to recognize the authority we have in Jesus, and to know who we are in the eyes of God: his children. The victory in these battles raging around us has already been won; it happened on the cross. We must not allow the enemy to take our eyes off the mission Jesus is leading us into, toward the lives he seeks to change.

That is what these attacks which manifest themselves in the physical realm are: attempts by our enemies in the spiritual realm to take our eyes off the *missio Dei*, the mission of God which he has placed on our lives. I know this seems simplistic, and it is. Friends, please listen to my warning. Dig into prayer, recognize the reality that we as church planters and pastors have stepped up to the front line of the battle, and the target Satan has placed on us, because we have choose to boldly follow God, under the guidance of Holy Spirit, into the mission field to see new churches form, and people's lives changed by the gospel. When we step up to push against the gates of

Hades, we are not making friends with Satan, but just the opposite. He will attack.

Truthfully you need to plan on moral, physical and/or financial attacks happening. For those of us who are married, Satan really likes to try to tear marriages apart. Be extra careful to focus on your spouse and resolve conflict quickly. I have seen marriages of ministry couples fail because they were not storm-proof. Satan seeks to hit us where it hurts most, and keeps coming back trying to hit the knockout punch. A few church plants later, and years since I learned this important reality, I can assure you that Satan is not creative. He doesn't have new schemes; he simply just keeps trying to hit us where we're most vulnerable, as a way to take your eyes off God, his gospel, and his desire to love others through you.

Another area of your life you need to shore up is your relationship with your kids (assuming you have some). Fatherhood (and motherhood) are under attack. Satan will try to take out your home life by stirring up your kids against you. He will try to derail their biblical understanding of the value of fathers. If he can succeed in taking away their appreciation of fatherhood in the physical realm, then it will adversely impact how they relate to God, their spiritual Father.

I find it curious that the times I have the most clarity in Bible study, when I'm the most mentally alert to give my time to God, is when my kids seem to act up the most. Some days I just have to reach out and touch my Bible as I get ready to read it, and one of my kids seems to go off the handle. (I am not suggesting all our kids are little demons, but some days it seems so.) If I act towards them in an ungraceful manner, then I am teaching my kids that God the Father is also not filled with grace.

Not only does Satan use our response to our kids as a way to manipulate our kids' understanding of fatherhood, he uses our kids to try and take our mind off Christ in the heat of spiritual moments. Please don't hear me saying that kids are a distraction, because kids are awesome. I love being a dad. I wouldn't trade this role in life for anything. But in those moments we need to exercise grace, because it alone will keep our homes solid, and keep our kids knowing that God as Father is a good thing.

If we allow these attacks to tear our family apart, then we can easily be taken out of the game and put on the bench until we can sort things out. Also as we model biblical fatherhood to our family, other families around us will see how good a Father God is. (Ironically as I write these words three of my kids are in the living room fighting over the X-box controller and which cartoon to watch on Netflix. And the littlest one is demanding more milk.)

Confront the demons that are trying to take you out. Understand and make use of the authority given to you by Jesus. The demons have no authority in your life unless you give it to them. You have authority over them. Command them to depart in the name of Jesus, because there truly is power in his name.[2] All the stories in the gospels of demonic attack, and demon possession are true; they are not fiction. It's not as I once assumed, that demons were something like Ghostbusters. This goes way beyond that little green ghost Slimer. Spiritual warfare is just as real today as it was for the prophets and apostles of the Bible.

Remember that Satan cannot stop the gospel from advancing, but he can try to create chaos and problems for those of us who are the hands and feet of Jesus, his

---

[2] Mississippi Baptist Convention Board, "Spiritual Warfare in Church Planting/Evangelism."

followers who are working to move the gospel forward, to see it change lives including our own.

Be on your toes, on the edge of your seat, waiting, knowing with expectation this will happen. Guard your hearts, turn inward to prayer. Know in the depths of your heart that you have authority over the situation, that God has given you power to trample on the demons.[3] Call on the name of Jesus. As Jesus himself reminds us, "These signs will follow those who believe, they will be able to cast out demons in my name."[4]

Paul writes, "I wouldn't want you to be ignorant of our history, brothers and sisters. Our ancestors were once safeguarded under a miraculous cloud in the wilderness and brought safely through the sea." This is an important reminder for us in dealing with the spiritual battles we will face. He tells us that the cloud was their protection. When we keep our eyes on the cloud, Holy Spirit, and rest in his presence, knowing He has already brought victory in our situation, we have nothing to fear.

---

[3] Romans 16:19, 20.

[4] Mark 16:17.

Remember, perfect love casts out all fear.[5] When we reside in that perfect love, there is truly no reason to fear whatever is currently trying to rock our boat, whatever is trying to take our eyes off the perfect love, Jesus. Keep your focus on Jesus as you move forward, as you press into the place he has called you to for the proclamation and living out of the gospel so that others will know Jesus is Lord, and faith communities will form. The cloud will guide you, and Holy Spirit will protect you on this pilgrimage.

---

[5] 1 John 4:18.

Chapter III: Pushing Forward

CHAPTER IV
You are a Child of God

Knowing you are a child of God is the most important aspect in moving forward. The gospel tells us we are his children, we have become co-heirs with Jesus. This is central to understanding the authority we have (which is given to us by Jesus), and from where all our ministry should be centered.

If we can come to understand this idea, this reality, on a heart level, then love will pour out unlike anything you can imagine, and unlike you have ever seen. Lives will be touched, and spiritual battles will be won. This is the reality of who we are. It's who God made us to be. We are His children.

"If you don't know the truth of who you are in Christ and if you don't know that you are seated in heavenly places (Ephesians 2:1-7, you should just read the whole chapter because it's awesome), then you are just a little boy shivering under his covers at night. But if you know what Jesus' sacrifice has won you, if you know even a piece of what God thinks about you, then you are the answer to every problem that crosses your path."[1]

I am not sure when I first truly understood this message, when it sunk to my heart level and became the reality that I live in daily. What I am certain of though are the results of knowing this truth. I have seen this truth change my life, alter my perspective, and change my worldview from one of sitting on the fence to seeing the world through the eyes of Jesus. Knowing that I am a child of God has instilled in me over time an understanding of the spiritual authority I have. With that in mind I have seen people healed and other miracles happen that resulted in the gospel being poured out in tangible ways into people's lives.

Knowing that I am a child of God has allowed me to fully embrace the truth and depth of knowing how much God loves me. It has been the central element in my

---

[1] Healy, *The Veil*, loc. 204.

pilgrimage of becoming more Christ-like, more of a "little Christ," a more mature Christian. The result was a breakthrough in my ministry, by allowing me to cast off the pride of holding onto titles and false expectations.

Confession: For years I worked hard to craft the most perfect and meaningful job title. I tried on Network Engineer, Corporate Bookkeeper, Consultant, Head Bicycle Mechanic, even Pastor. I was seeking to be significant in people's eyes. I wanted to gain approval, to have status, and be near the top of the food chain.

What I have learned is that striving after titles to gain approval from others and to be someone important is like throwing chaff into the wind. It's pointless. A thought that keep reoccurring to me is, "Will my job title comfort me on my death bed?" The truth is that it's very unlikely. When I breath my last, no one will care if I was a CEO, a janitor, a pastor, or whatever. What will be most important will be knowing that God smiles upon me and calls me his child.

I can waste my entire life trying to gain approval from those around me, but that really doesn't matter. I could also waste my life trying to gain God's approval, but that would only be empty religion. Why? Simply because I already have God's approval. He calls me his child, his beloved, his bride.

There is nothing I can do to gain or lose his approval. He looks down and smiles on me. This is true for you too. You and I are made in God's image, and we are his children. "Child of God": that is the only title or label that matters.

In the last chapter we briefly looked at spiritual warfare. Knowing that we are God's children is an important component of the spiritual battles you will face in developing communities of "little Christs" gathered together to grow in faith and worship God. When you truly get this on a heart level, that you are a child of God, you will understand the authority given to you, and that because you are his child, God has already placed the victory in your hands.

"For all who did receive and trust in Him, he gave them the right to be reborn as Children of God."[2]

"Through that prayer, God's Spirit confirms in our spirits that we are His children."[3]

---

[2] John 1:12.

[3] Romans 8:16.

"Consider the kind of extravagant love the Father has lavished on us – He calls us children of God! It's true; we are His beloved children. And in the same way the world didn't recognize Him, the world does not recognize us either. My loved ones, we have been adopted into God' family; and we are officially His children now."[4]

These verses are just a few of many that confirm to us we are his children. I encourage you to take time to meditate on these truths. Let them sink into your heart. Let God whisper them to your spirit. (We will learn more in the next chapter about hearing the voice of God.) I know I keep repeating myself, but it's to signify the importance of this word, and the truth that it holds for your life, so that it goes deep inside you. When you live in and know the reality of being God's child, you will experience victory, you will see breakthroughs, and you will see the love of God pour out from you unlike anything you have known before, and lives, communities, villages, cities will change.

Simply put, to really know this will give you a firm footing on which to stand and face any spiritual fight that comes your way, whether it be in church planting

---

[4] 1 John 3:1, 2.

and any other ministry endeavor in your life, including personal growth in faith. I want you to know without a doubt that because God has given you victory, there is no need to worry, no need to feel defeated, and that you have every reason to believe that God will push back the walls of Hades and open the doors he has promised to open in the territory he has brought you to.

Tied into knowing you are a child of God is casting off the label of "sinner," and embracing the reality that God sees you as pure and holy, complete, the image of Christ. Repeat to yourself: "I am a sinner saved by grace, but more importantly, I now am God's child, a new creation reborn in his image by the transforming power of Jesus."

What a radical shift in thinking! It seems we are always chanting the first part ("I am a sinner saved by grace.") We take pride in this, but in fact it is a lie, because once you confess Jesus as Lord and Savior and become his disciple, you are no longer a sinner, you are a new creation. He no longer considers you as a sinner; he calls you his brother or sister, while Father God sees you as his child. You have been reborn, renewed, transformed into the holy and perfect image of God. You have become the person God designed you to be. Yes, there is still work to be done in the physical realm, but when

God looks down at you, he smiles, because he sees you as his perfect child.

Praise God for his grace that saved me and made me a new creation! Praise God for the transforming power that raised me from the grave and the bondage of sin, into a new life! God has made us whole and fully human, once more. We are restored, reborn, renewed in the image of Christ.

How we label ourselves will either impede or advance our spiritual and physical life (not that they should be separate, but we often compartmentalize them). Words are powerful. James wrote that our words are like sparks that can set an entire forest ablaze, or like a rudder that can turn a ship around. In the same way, we need to be careful in the choice of words we assign to ourselves. See yourself as you really are: a beloved child of God, a new creation.

Cast off your old ways, and be renewed in your mind. When we recognize that we have been made new, our past life as a sinner is behind us and a new future lies ahead. Step into the reality of who you are in Jesus, and how God sees you. Remind yourself that you are a new creation. It is important to do this until you fully actualize this reality in your life. Jesus has made you whole, you just need to step into your wholeness. As his brother and sister, you are a co-heirs with him of the kingdom of God.[5]

As you step out into this new understanding, it will also change how you share the gospel with others. It will change your goals as a planter from building a not-for-profit organization that tries to speak into a neighborhood toward seeing the gospel impact lives and renew communities. That's because this message of being a child of God is not just for you, it's for all those you come in contact with. As you change your title from pastor/planter to child of God, those around you will see God's love in you, and they will want more of more of God themselves. And as a community of Jesus followers begins to grow, you will begin to see others come alongside and journey with you. This is how to impact the city you are in. It's the love of Jesus, and living out of who our Father made us to be.

---

[5] Romans 8:17.

CHAPTER V

Hearing the Voice of God

The boy Samuel continued to serve the Eternal One under the guidance of Eli. In those days, messages from the Eternal were rare, and sacred dreams or visions were given to very few. Eli, who was very old, had become almost blind. He was lying in his room, it was late at night but before dawn as the lamp of God still burned. Samuel was resting in the house of the Eternal One, where the covenant chest of the True God was located, and he heard a voice.

Eternal One: Samuel! Samuel!

Samuel: Here I am (running to Eli)I heard you calling; here I am.

Eli: I did not call you, my son. Go back, and lie down.

So Samuel went back to bed. But the Eternal called him again.

Eternal One: Samuel!

Samuel (running to Eli):; I heard you calling here I am!

Eli: No, I did not call you, my son. Go back and lie down, I need my rest.

Samuel did not recognize the voice of the Eternal One, for the word of the Eternal had not been revealed to Samuel yet. So Samuel went back again to his bed. And the Eternal One called him a third time.

Samuel (running to Eli): I know you called me; I am here!

Eli (realizing the Lord was calling Samuel): Go back and lie down, my son. If the voice calls you again, I want you to say, "Speak, Eternal One. Your servant is listening."

So Samuel went to his bed in his place and listened. Then the Eternal One came into his presences as before.

Eternal One: Samuel! Samuel!

Samuel: Speak, Eternal One. Your servant is listening. [1]

Are we any different? We are so used to taking steps on our own, to moving forward so fast that we do not take the time to recognize when in fact the voice of God is calling us. Sometimes we may not even know how to hear the voice of God when he calls out to us. This is an especially important part of our pilgrimage as we move into missional roles and look to God to find out where he is already working in our cities, and whose lives he is speaking into.

It is critical that we be able to discern his voice from the others around us. Much like in our discussion in a previous chapter on spiritual warfare, we need to discern

---

[1] 1 Samuel 3:1-10.

when it might be demons who are speaking, trying to lead us off course. Thus we need to know how to test the voices speaking to us, and with certainty know the voice of God when he calls out.

Jesus: My sheep respond as the hear My voice; I know them intimately, and they follow me. [2]

This is how it should be for us: God speaks, we respond. Intimacy is the key to knowing the voice of God within us. We need to be spending time with God, and learning to hear him exclusively. We need to know clearly that it is he who is speaking to us. One of the tools that I had learned early on for testing the spirits speaking to me was simply to ask them, "Do you confess Jesus as Lord and Savior?" If they say yes, then certainly it is God speaking. But the voices who tell you no, clearly are not. Demonic voices are seeking to send you off course and will not to say yes to this question. They cannot say yes since Jesus is not their Lord. To them Satan is lord, he is who they are aligned with and follow.

"My loved ones, I warn you: do not trust every spirit. Instead, examine them carefully to determine if they come from God, because the corrupt world is filled with

---

[2] John 10:27.

voices of many false prophets. Here is how you know God's Spirit; if a spirit affirms the truth that Jesus the Anointed, our Liberating King, has come in human flesh, then that spirit is from God. If a spirit does not affirm the true nature of Jesus the Anointed, then that spirit does not come from God and is, in fact, the spirit of the anti-Christ."[3]

This idea holds biblical weight; it is wisdom God gave us through John to teach us how to know God's voice. This will always be a valuable tool to have on your belt, but only as you spend more and more time listening to and getting to know the voice of God. Intimacy will develop, and you will be able to discern faster, and come to a point where you simply know that it is God speaking to you. At this point, though, many of us are like Samuel, and not as familiar with the voice of God speaking to us as we should be. Therefore, it would be wise to take time to test the spirit behind every message we receive.

Half the battle of hearing from God is knowing when you're actually listening to yourself. The other half is faith. We need to have faith to trust that the revelation we are receiving is from God, and the faith to put it into action. The more we do this the more our faith grows,

---

[3] 1 John 4:1-3.

the more we know we are hearing God's voice instead of our own. We need to flex our faith muscles. It is very similar to going to a gym. If you want to have a fit body with protruding muscles you put in hours working out and lifting weights. Over time muscles will develop. It's the same spiritual matters. If you want to grow in faith you need to flex your faith muscles and work to develop them. It takes time, it takes practice, it is hard work, but as you train and grow, so will your faith.

I can remember times when I knew God was stirring my family to move to another city. I would not jump into action directly. I'd bring together people I trusted to pray into the idea and hear what they also were hearing. One of the hardest times was leaving the church I was planting in Halifax, Nova Scotia, to make a move to Winnipeg, Manitoba. There was a nudging in my spirit, I knew God was telling us to do this. It was a challenging choice to make, only two years into our church plant and knowing it would dissolve when my wife and I left. But God wanted us to move. So we talked to the elders of our church, and some other leaders around us whom we trusted, and shared the idea. They prayed with us. I tested the spirit behind the word myself, asking if it was of God and if the one speaking confessed Jesus as Lord and Savior. It worked. One housemate (we lived in a communal house) shared with us a dream he had had of our family moving away to Winnipeg. I had not even told them what I had heard from God. But God spoke through him as confirmation of the words we received and the plan God had. I knew God's voice, I was confident in that. But it was important to have this confirmation. Especially with such a large decision at stake. After a lot of prayer we began the process of seeing our church plant come to a close, and we made the move to Winnipeg.

A surefire way to know if we have been hearing from God is to look at the fruit in our lives. The outcome of the words we hear will be bound in love, filled with grace, encouraging, and move a person or a group of people closer to God. The fruit of the spirit will be present in what is said.

In a similar way, the beautiful part of trusting God is seeing the fruit of the words and guidance you've received from God. Such was the case with the church plant we closed when we heard God was shifting us to a new place. Most of the people entrusted in our care moved on, they regained a love for the church that had faded away, and we were able to help them transition to new churches where they built great relationships and grew in their faith. This is something that would not have happened early in the church plant because we were all broken, disgruntled with church as usual, and in need of healing. This was the fruit of it all-- those great people we had the privilege to love for two years were healthy again and becoming active members in the Christian communities around them.

As we grow closer to God, we will know his voice more. The still, silent whisper will become louder and more familiar. Like the sheep, we will know our Shepherd's voice. We will know when God speaks to us and calls us to action. We need to be willing to develop our faith muscles and grow spiritually. But beyond knowing when we hear God speaking, we also need the faith to trust what he is saying to us and to follow through on them. Just like anything, this takes practice. Sometimes we will mess up, but we need to see our mistakes not as failures (do not let the evil spirits whisper this lie to you), but rather as an opportunity to see where we went wrong, to turn back to God and dig deeper. Soon our stumbling like a toddler taking her first awkward steps will turn into walking. In time, we will be running marathons with God as we exercise our faith more and more.

We will recognize the voice of God sooner and more intimately as we grow in faith. I have faith in you that you already hear God's voice and are used to operating by his word, following his cloud, Holy Spirit. Some of us may not know how to label that experience, and yet we operate in it and know with an assurance from deep inside us that the words are God's, the direction is His, and that the words given to us for others are from him.

I recall when I first heard with clarity words from Holy Spirit. I had know idea what was happening, and I had no words to express what I was sensing. I have had many Holy Spirit encounters of God pursuing me, but I have had no frame of reference for any of them. Yet God was faithful; he kept speaking and kept trying to grab my heart. Then one day I got it. I knew his voice. Like Samuel I had someone tell me it was God speaking, and that maybe I should listen to him and tell him I am willing to hear his words and obey.

As you learn to obey the revelations from Holy Spirit, your faith will grow more, and your relationship deepen. When you take time to stop, discern, push aside other voices and say, "I'm here, Lord. Speak to me," you will be amazed what God has to say to you, and you will see your faith grow each time you do this. Please be patient, as this will not happen overnight. Nor will usually happen instantly as we've come to expect from our microwaves and the Internet. (It sure did not happen like that for me!) But I assure you that as you draw close to God, as you listen to His still, small voice, you will learn to know without doubt the voice of your Shepherd.

CHAPTER VI

Philip and the Ethiopian

A heavenly messenger brought this short message from the Lord to Philip during his time preaching in Samaria:

Messenger of the Lord: Leave Samaria. Go south to the Jerusalem-Gaza road.

The message was especially unusual because this road runs through the middle of uninhabited desert. But Philip got up, left the excitement of urban Samaria, and did as he was told. [1]

What happens next is an amazing divine appointment. Philip heard the voice of God, knew without a doubt

---

[1] Acts 8:26, 27.

that it was God, and obeyed. As a result a man's heart was filled with joy to overflowing, and he wanted to get baptized immediately. It's conceivable that because of this fellow was a eunuch, he held a place of importance, a place where his words and deeds affected the lives of others. We could easily presume that because of his joy in his newfound faith in Jesus, he impacted the lives of many others in the queen's household, and that they too made decisions for Jesus.

Simply put, because Philip was willing and open to Holy Spirit speaking to him, and guiding his pilgrimage to spread the gospel, lives were changed. This is how it should be for us too; we should be in a place where we are willing to allow Holy Spirit to be interrupt us, to change our course and direct us to where God wants us to go, and to speak to those whom God wants us to speak.

I had a "Philip moment" in my life. I was the "eunuch", a recipient of a word from a man lead by God. It was a point in my life when I had run away from the church, pushed back against God, and tried to be as un-Christ-like as I could. I was a pastor's kid. I had grown up in church, and I had read the Bible all my life. The love and grace of God should not have been foreign to me. But the gospel had not truly become personal to me; it had not traveled the long road from my head to my heart. Sure, I confessed my faith a thousand times and went to the front at altar calls during youth conferences. It became routine to respond to altar calls, to read my Bible (and beat myself up for slipping up in doing daily devotions when I didn't). Yet when I got out on my own when I was 17, I went wild at the idea of being my own person.

After a couple years of running from church and God, Sundays were still a day of rest, but mostly because I was nursing hangovers. There I was a pilgrim in life trying to move forward to a new destination, desperately in need of the gospel, but I had ran away from it. I had just enrolled to take a program in computer-related studies, and working hard to move forward. It all seemed overwhelming.

I was sitting on a park bench pondering life after just having enrolled in an expensive private college. Suddenly a man, we'll call him Philip, strolled up, put his hand on my shoulder and spoke gospel words to me. "God wants you back, he misses you. This time it's going to be better." My Philip heard a word from God, which he had the bravado to follow the prompting of Holy Spirit to come share it with me. This man likely did not know how much his words would pierce my heart, or that I would run home and get on my knees later that day. But because of him being willing to share with me a word that he heard from God, I stopped running from God; I realized I needed him. God moved me toward reconciling with my parents and with others I knew I had hurt as a result of how I was living. More importantly I could hear clearly the call on my life to become a pastor (which was actually part of the reason I tried to run from God), and eventually I began pushing toward that goal. But not a single piece of this would have happened, if my Philip had not taken the time to open up the gospel to me. Who knows where my life would have ended up, were it not for him? Would the people I've had the privilege to share the gospel with have ever come to faith in Christ?

The apostle Philip had no idea when he stepped out in faith and followed through with the prompting from Holy Spirit the impact his words would make. What he knew was God wanted him to speak with that eunuch, so he did. He shared the gospel with that man sitting in his chariot. As a result, a life was changed, a household was likely changed, and possibly because of his position of authority in his country, he helped turn a nation toward God. On arriving back home, the eunuch, with love pouring out from his heart, shared the gospel with others, all because Philip was willing to take action on a word from God.

As we move forward in church planting, this is without question how we should go, to be willing to follow the promptings of the voice of God within us. His promptings are not a disruption to our lives, they are life, because they call us to action through faith.

I can think of a time in my own life when after a couple years of living in one city, we had decided to commit to a couple more years to really dig in and forge a community around us. However God had different plans for us. He wanted us to go back to my home city, Halifax, Nova Scotia, and plant a church there. I was honestly initially resistant to this idea. I knew we would be going there in a few years, and we weren't prepared for it to be right then. My wife and I had just chatted about digging deeper into Edmonton, where we lived at the time, and trying to make a go of life there. I had just started a great job as a bicycle mechanic in a really awesome shop. But God's voice was loud and clear for us to go *now*.

I took time to pray with others, and seek confirmation of the word, to discern that I was truly hearing God correctly. Confirmation after confirmation poured into our lives. One of the boldest was when we received notice that we had 90 days to either put a down payment on our apartment, because our building was being sold as condos, or move out. We searched for a new place to live in Edmonton but the doors closed quickly. We could not find a new home there. This was one of many things that happened that showed us God was clearly saying it time to move back to Halifax and plant a church.

It was settled. The date was set, plane tickets were bought (which was an amazing God-provision, especially given how cheap the tickets were). Most of our possessions were sold to pay for the move. With twelve boxes of our most essential belongings (including my bikes and tools!), and a six-month-old son in our arms, we boarded a plane out of obedience to God's calling. We landed in the early morning in Halifax, rented a van, and dug into to a new life. Within hours of landing, God provided us with a home, and a few days later I had a job in my field as a bicycle mechanic (another miracle since unemployment was high in Halifax at the time).

As well, we knew God was calling us back to what I regarded as my home church. That allowed us to speak and share about God's desire for us to start a church community that looked nothing like "church as usual," which in turn lead us to recruit some key leadership members for our eventual church plant. (Let me be clear: I do not endorse sheep-stealing, but if God is speaking to others to be part of a core church-planting team, that is different.)

Within a period of a few months after landing in Halifax we saw a community form around us. We met regularly several times a week to share meals and resources, and to pour love into the neighborhoods around us. It all happened because we were faithful to listening to Holy Spirit to guide our steps. We saw his interruption of our lives as a call to action, and as a result lives where changed. Jesus said, "Follow me," and we did.

I believe God has divine appointments for all of us, much like he did and continues to for me, much like he did for Philip. We need to be wise in listening to the voice of Holy Spirit, discerning in testing the spirits, and willing to take the steps to move to where we are being sent and to who we are to speak to. Some of us may not see churches birthed (that is not meant to be discouraging, just truthful), but we will see lives impacted by the gospel, often in ways we cannot even imagine.

I have often lived by the principle and challenge that God can and will do more then I can ask or imagine.[2] I've always thought I have a huge imagination, and yet God has done amazing things beyond even what I could imagine, He has impacted many lives in ways I would have thought impossible, because I was faithful to his words. I have absolute certainty in my heart that many of you have similar stories, stories of times when you felt a nudge from God to speak to someone, and because you spoke to them, they were blessed, they felt and heard the gospel, and the presence of the kingdom shone around them. Maybe as a result of you stepping out and trusting the words you heard, communities were blessed and moved closer towards God, possibly even entire cities were impacted as well. We may never know this side of heaven what kind of impact we've had, but what matters now is that you, like Phillip, be willing to respond to God.

---

[2] Ephesians 3:20.

CHAPTER VII
Pilgrims Not Tourists

When we enter a new place we like to look around and check out the scenery. Some of us may pull out guide books to find out where we may want to go. There are landmarks, museums, possibly waterfront vendors, and many touristy things that can catch our attention. Sporting our clearly not local attire we wander about trying to form an impression based on tour guides, signs, and souvenir shops. After a few hours, having collected lots of brochures and some tourist-y shirts that proudly display the name of the place, we think we may have a grasp of the place. We begin to convince ourselves we understand its culture, its people, its economy. Yet the truth is we do not have a clue as to what the area is actually about; what we have is a kind of a movie trailer impression based on what a few local vendors and the tourist bureau have told us. We're still visiting foreigners, and the locals know it.

One of our greatest challenges when going to a new place is to become a pilgrim not a tourist. Tourists are not interested in building into a local area, they come with a mindset to consume all that they can in a short period of time, and then leave. A pilgrim goes to a place and seeks to be immersed in its culture and to experience life as it's lived there. Pilgrims set up homes and dig in to bless their new community. Tourists pass through a place and it stays the same. Pilgrims, on the other hand, are changed by engaging with the locals, they are deeply affected and challenged by the local culture and crave to be part of it.

Early Celtic Christians left their homes to venture to an unknown destination guided by, and with complete trust, in divine providence. Their journeys often lead to the development of new places of worship and the spread of Christianity to pagan areas.[1]

As pilgrims enter a place, they enter the topography of faith. There are non-Christians, pre-Christians, nominal believers, and those who are mature in faith. Our key

---

[1] Wikimedia Foundation, LLC, "Pilgrim."

expectation under guidance of Holy Spirit is to be accepting of each other's diversity, accepting where each person is at in their faith, and to become one body together moving toward a greater relationship with God. We can only do that if we come with a pilgrim mindset. Tourists arrive, take in the sights and whatever else is offered them, and then leave. Pilgrims, on the other hand, roll up their sleeves and get to work alongside Holy Spirit, to see transformation come about for the sake of the kingdom of God in the lives of the people around them. Pilgrims invest their lives alongside the community that already exists.

A fine example of this life-investment comes from the Anabaptist faith and story into which my own life has been grafted. My Mennonite forefathers were offered free land in rural Manitoba on condition they managed within three to five years to turn the land into valuable homesteads. If they were successful, they would be given title to the land.

Under God's direction, these hard-working folks came to this new place. As pilgrims, they walked the land, learned about it, and tilled the soil. They knew God had given them the land, and that it was their responsibility to see it become valuable farmland. And they did. Now where there was once swamp are massive dikes and irrigation systems which they built that have transformed it into beautiful farms. Towns have also grown up and flourished.

This is what we are called to as church planters, to become pilgrims to the land. Roll up our sleeves and till the soil. Not only are we investing physically alongside others, we are digging in spiritually. This spiritual soil will be tilled, the seed of the gospel will be planted, and the fruit of the Spirit will grow rapidly. Over time, under the guidance of Holy Spirit, we will see where the harvest is, and we will see the flags of the kingdom of God raised up. Communities of believers will grow and flourish.

"This is what the Eternal, Commander of heavenly armies and God of Israel, says to those He exiles from Jerusalem to Babylon: Build houses - make homes for your families because you are not coming back to Judah anytime soon. Plant gardens, and eat the food you grow there. Marry and have children; find wives for yours sons, and give our daughters in marriage, so that they can have children. During these years of captivity, let your families grow and not die out. Pursue the peace and welfare of the city where I sent you into exile. Pray to Me, the

Eternal, for Babylon because if it has peace, you will live in peace."[2]

Although we are not exiles like the nation of Israel was, we are lead by Holy Spirit to where he wants us to be. We are called to seek peace and welfare, to build homes, dig gardens, marry, and to build into the culture in which we are living. Holy Spirit guides each step, divine providence creates each relationship, each fruit of our labors we taste is a gift from God. As we orient ourselves towards the work that God is leading us to, as we take his hand, and follow in his footsteps, the peace and the welfare of our community will blossom. God is at work already in the places where he sends us. As pilgrims, it is our challenge to go to that place, to grow in it, and to live and walk under the guidance of God, leading others closer to Him. If we go and try to reinvent the wheel, so to speak, we will miss the mark. If we go in with our ideas, our planting kits and formulas, and try to do what worked for others in other places, we will fail to discern God's plan for reaching that area. But if we go in and follow God's direction, as imparted to us by his Spirit, then we will see our faith communities flourish, we will see lives impacted, and we will see the fruit of the Spirit take root and change the faith landscape. The light of

---

[2] Jeremiah 29:5-7.

God's kingdom will overwhelm and transform the topography of faith, and light will flood the darkest valleys.

"Go out and make disciples in all the nations. Ceremonially wash them through baptism in the name of the triune God: Father, Son and Holy Spirit. Then disciple them. Form them in the practices and postures that I have taught you, and show them how to follow the commands I have laid down for you."[3]

---

[3] Matthew 28:19, 20.

AFTERWORD

My friends, I hope that in some way what you've read here will help convince you hat we need to get back to the basics. We—I include myself in this—must put aside our fancy strategies, our own ideas, and cast our eyes again on the One who called us into the missional journeys we are embarking on. It is God's mission (*missio dei*) we are joining in on, so it is to him we should turn; it is he we should listen to and follow.

We need to stop trying, as it were, to steer a cruise ship into port with a flashlight, and start allowing the Light of the world to be our guide, to be our everything. God already has a perfect plan in place for how to reach out with the gospel to the people and the places to which he has called us. It would be harmful if we went in with our own preconceived ideas or strategies that have worked elsewhere, thinking we had the answers. Only God has the answers that we need to hear, and he is happy to reveal them to us. We simply need to take time to listen to him.

I know it is a struggle to not look at models that have grown churches, and in some cases very quickly. I catch myself at times stargazing whenever I watch videos of people I'll call superstar pastors. I recall going to a popular conference on church planting. I was so caught up in the excitement that I came away with the idea that if I followed steps A through Z, I would have a massive mega-church within two years. I quickly realized this was not how it actually was going to be, that this is not what we are called to.

The truth is that even those mega-churches took decades to grow. Their pastors moved to a place, dug in with both feet in prayer, and followed through with how God planned to reach that place. They took the time to know the voice and heed of God, and have the bravado in faith to put his steps in place. What we see now is the fruit of hard work, lots of time on their knees, and years of perseverance in following the cloud.

We have the cloud of God, Holy Spirit, within us. God placed him in us upon our confession of faith in Jesus. As people baptized in the Spirit, God is constantly speaking to us, and we need to learn to listen. Call out, "Here I am, Lord!" We need to put aside us, and put on Him. "Let Jesus Christ be as near to you as the clothes you wear."[1] John the Baptist said of Jesus, "He must increase, I must decrease."[2] That needs to hold true for us as well: he must take over our lives, we must diminish. That needs to be our reality as we seek to push forward the kingdom forward. We need as well to know the mind of Christ, which Holy Spirit will reveal to us.

My greatest hope for you is that you have heard the voice of God, taken time to seek him out and be in his presence. God calls out for us to "Be still and know that I am Lord"[3] From a place of resting in God, you will hear him, and you will be able to clearly discern the pilgrimage God has in place for you to draw people together, to be the church together, and to successfully move towards forming a faith community of disciples, seeking to hear and know God's voice, and to follow him

---

[1] Romans 13:14. CEV.

[2] John 3:30.

[3] Psalm 46:10.

into the collective mission he is calling you to. Then more disciples will come into a deep relationship with God and go where he sends them. I pray that you will become communities of disciples that reproduce more disciples, and those disciples will go on to form new communities that reflect the kingdom of God here on earth.

God is everywhere and the harvest is plentiful. It is up to us to take the time to listen to the voice of God, and follow through on whatever commands he is giving us. God is calling you back to him; he wants to spread his love over you and deep into your soul. Then he wants to send you, his child, out into the fields to gather the harvest.

Are you willing to set aside everything and follow God's perfect plans? Are you willing to let go of the false security you have in your and other people's plans and agendas, and trust God, to comes alongside him to plant the church that will reach the unique group of people he has sent you to?

I assure you if you are, it will be an amazing pilgrimage. It will bless you more than anything you could ever ask for or imagine. God loves you more than you know. He wants the blessings he's ready to bestow on you to bear much fruit. You simply have to say yes.

Afterword

BIBLIOGRAPHY

Brister, Tim. "5 Simple Ways to Move from Strangers to
    Missionaries. *Verge Network,* September 2, 2013.
    Online: http://www.vergenetwork.org/
    2013/09/02/5-simple-ways-to-move-people-from-
    strangers-to-missionaries/.
Halter, Hugh. *The Tangible Kingdom: Creating
    Incarnational Community.* San Francisco: Jossey-
    Bass, 2012.
Healy, Blake. *The Veil.* The Veil, 2008.
Mississippi Baptist Convention Board. "Spiritual
    Warfare in Church Planting/Evangelism." Online:
    http://www.mbcb.org/download/cp/7steps/1/
    Spiritual%20Warfare.pdf.
Stetzer, Ed. "Do Not Plant or Pastor a Church in Your
    Head." *Christianity Today,* May 18, 2010. Online:
    http://www.christianitytoday.com/edstetzer/2010/
    may/do-not-plant-or-pastor-church-in-your-
    head.html.
Surratt, Greg. "The Danger of Planting Lego Churches."
    Pastors.com. Online: http://pastors.com/lego-church/.

Wikimedia Foundation, LLC. "Pilgrim." *Wikipedia.*
Online: http://en.wikipedia.org/wiki/Pilgrim.

ABOUT THE AUTHOR

Paul lives in one of the most amazing regions of Canada, the Okanagan Valley. There he mountain bikes on rugged mountainous terrain, enjoys fly fishing in remote alpine lakes, and teaches his four children the joys of God's creation through outdoor adventures and urban farming. His passion runs deep for the church and to see new expressions of the church come alive to reach out to those who normally would not attend church.

He has lived across Canada in various cities and been deeply involved in church planting in the urban context. Paul is currently in the infancy stages of developing a church and ministry in his new home town, Vernon, British Columbia. He hopes to see the gospel impact lives daily on the streets of his city and to lead disciples towards doing that as well.

Paul has a diverse background in Computer Science, Business Administration and has dabbled in religious studies with a focus on Islam.

ABOUT ULP

Urban Loft Publishers focuses on ideas, topics, themes, and conversations about all things urban. Renewing the city is the central theme and focus of what we publish. It is our intention to blend urban ministry, theology, urban planning, architecture, urbanism, stories, and the social sciences, as ways to drive the conversation. While we lean towards scholarly and academic works, we explore the fun and lighter sides of cities as well. We publish a wide variety of urban perspectives, from books by the experts about the city to personal stories and personal accounts of urbanites who live in the city.

www.theurbanloft.org
@the_urban_loft

OTHER BOOKS BY ULP

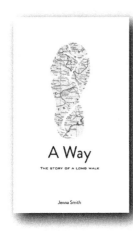

A Way: The Story of a Long Walk
Jenna Smith

But why? Why would a young urbanite leave the comforts of home and walk 65 days through rain and hail and scorching sun? So begins *A Way*, the recounting of a young woman's pilgrimage along the Camino di Santiago from France through Spain, with nothing more than the bag on her back and her husband by her side. It tells of the people met (the quirky ones, the lost ones, the kind and unforgettable ones), the physical discomforts endured (and oh, how many there were) and of the road travelled (all 1065 miles of it). It reveals how a sacred pilgrimage can bring about the most unsacred of experiences. It is a memoir, intertwined with reflections from the walking and lessons learned on the road about time, about the body, and about community. But most of all, it's a story. The story of a long walk.

No Home Like Place: A Christian Theology of Place
Leonard Hjalmarson

"The sense of being lost, displaced, and homeless is pervasive in contemporary culture. The yearning to belong somewhere, to be in a safe place, is a deep and moving pursuit. Loss of place and yearning for place are dominant images ..." (Brueggemann, *The Land*)

Fragmentation, mobility, dualism—these forces work against our belonging, and work against our richly dwelling in the places we live. Add to these the rise of "virtual" place and relationships, and our sense of displacement only increases. It has been difficult to embrace a call to life as mission in this world under these conditions, and equally difficult to embrace a call to place.

Are there "sacred" places? If every place is sacred, does the word lose its meaning? What is it that God loves about place? Can architecture contribute to our ability to engage in a place? How do experiential human questions like "belonging" intersect with a theological lens? Does a biblical view of place imply an ecology and an ethic? How do pilgrimage and place relate? How can the arts assist us in place-making? This book addresses these questions and more, in a lively dialogue between theology and culture.

The Communal Imagination: Finding a Way to Share Life Together
Mark Votava

Everyday life is often times not experienced as very relational anymore. The church has been co-opted by services and meetings detached from a relational expression within a particular place or parish in everyday life. We need to create the context to reimagine the body of Christ in everyday life as embodied through its proximity and shared life together. Without the value of inhabiting and listening to the place where we live, we will have very little expression of faith together in everyday life. There needs to be an embodied expression for our ecclesiology to make sense. If we do not have a local expression together, we will create a duality between our spirituality and our everyday lives in the ordinary. *The Communal Imagination* will draw out a new way of being for ourselves into this transition of embodied expression by stressing the importance of proximity and shared life within a particular neighborhood where we live, work and play. We need to embody practices as a way of life that are based on a spirituality of love, grace, humility and simplicity within the place where we share life together. This is how we will be able to get along and function in a healthy way over time that does not do damage to the cultural context we are in as we build on the particulars of our relationships together.

Made in the USA
Middletown, DE
06 March 2022

62239360R00060